Organising Idea No. 1

A monograph published for the
EUROPEAN THERAPY STUDIES INSTITUTE

Hypnosis and trance states
A new psychobiological explanation

HG Publishing for
The European Therapy Studies Institute
Chalvington, Hailsham, East Sussex BN27 3TD, United Kingdom

Printed in Great Britain

ISBN 1 899398 90 2

Hypnosis and trance states
A new psychobiological explanation

"A man who carries his own lantern
does not fear darkness."

Saying

Organising Ideas

"All scientific knowledge is a correlation of *what* is seen
with the *way* that it is seen."

Henri Bortoft, *The Wholeness of Nature*

In all fields confusion flourishes, mistakes are made and
harm is done when we forget that the *way* we look at
something is dependent on an active effort of imagination
and thinking. We are not mechanical recording instruments
looking out on a fixed world (although this is certainly the
philosophy of science which is usually communicated by the
way science is taught in schools, presented in popular books
and revealed in television programmes). We *organise* what
we see through what we believe we know.

When a field of study is confused about something, it
usually needs a new organising idea.

An organising idea plays an active role in shaping our
perception, thinking and research and is always larger than
earlier ideas because it has to explain the anomalies that
previously caused confusion.

This paper, one of a series commissioned by the European
Therapy Studies Institute, offers a new organising idea.

ETSI 2001

*To our families, friends
and colleagues.*

Hypnosis and trance states
A new psychobiological explanation

Joseph Griffin and Ivan Tyrrell

"A theory is the more impressive the greater the simplicity of its premises, the more different kinds of things it relates, and the more extended its area of applicability."

Albert Einstein

Hypnosis and trance states
A new psychobiological explanation

A LONG TIME ago, in the heat and dust of a famous battle, a man had his leg chopped off with a mighty blow from an unusual double pointed sword. Without hesitation, he picked up his leg and threw it at his enemy.[1] How could that happen?

We all love a mystery, a puzzle, something to solve. If the mystery has exotic or bizarre elements to it, so much the better. Human beings in trance states clearly exhibit strange behaviours that have fascinated people since the dawn of self-awareness. These behaviours include: a massive increase in susceptibility to suggestion, great tolerance of painful procedures (skin piercing, burning), religious conversions, hallucinations, indoctrination, age regression, profound stillness, and the opposite – super physical performance. In trance amnesia can be induced, creativity stimulated, blood flow altered, the immune system boosted, major operations – including amputations – undergone without pain and skin conditions cured or created (stigmata for example). Moods can be changed, depressed people can laugh again and over-whelming fears can be faced and overcome. And, under hypnosis, strange transformations of character can occur: shy people can become confident, inhibited people turn into sexual exhibitionists and cowards discover bravery.

Trance can be induced in numerous ways: by drugs, music, rhythmic dancing, rituals, shock, hypnotic language, touch, sexual activity, reflection, staring at a scene, recalling particular memories, stories, changing breathing patterns, and anything that arouses strong emotion. It is, therefore, a common everyday experience. Yet it is still mysterious, almost invisible to most people. The history of hypnosis has had a rocky ride over thousands of years – accepted in some cultures, banned in others. Down the ages its use has been associated with great therapeutic benefits (which it undoubtedly can confer), but also with severe warnings about the dangers (which we think are real) that its use can put both the hypnotic subject *and* the hypnotist in. However, in all its long history there has never been a clear explanation of what is going on that modern science can work from.

How can a state so easy to observe, and that can be induced in so many, often apparently contradictory, ways, be so little understood? Some scientists even doubt its reality.

An article published in the *New Scientist*[2] usefully summarises the current debate as to whether hypnosis as a trance state exists. The article reduced the debate to "two sides". One side seems to show that there is increasing evidence that hypnosis is an altered state of consciousness. Its proponents nowadays produce dramatic PET scans showing that brain activity is altered when people are given suggestions under hypnosis that they are not experiencing pain or that they can see something that is not there – an hallucination. Good studies show quite clearly that, when hypnotised, the appropriate parts of the brain are activated whilst people respond to such suggestions.[3] There is a great difference between a person in hypnosis who can activate the parts of his brain that can switch off pain and somebody pretending their pain does not exist. PET scans show this.

The other side, the people who argue that hypnosis doesn't exist, say about these studies that, "this is not evidence because all it shows is that people are responding to suggestions. What you are actually measuring is suggestibility, not an altered state of consciousness."

Let's deal with this argument first. What criteria would satisfy such people that hypnosis actually exists? The answer is: none. This is because they are looking for a state of consciousness that cannot be accessed by any means other than hypnosis. And, if the brain is not behaving in an abnormal fashion when someone is hypnotised, they could never bring themselves to agree that hypnosis is happening. This is a logical absurdity.

We agree that hypnosis is not an altered state of consciousness if that means that the brain never functions that way other than when it is in an hypnotic state. We will also show that hypnosis *does* exist and that it is a naturally occurring state of mind that people dip in and out of, to varying extents, all the time.

To unwrap and explore the implications of this – which extend even as far as our knowledge of the evolution of consciousness – we need to start with a definition.

First things first

We define a trance state, as do many others, as a focused state of attention in which wider environmental stimuli are ignored. "There are many ways of inducing a trance", said the great, innovative psychiatrist, Milton H. Erickson. "What you do is ask patients primarily to give their attention to one particular idea. You get them to centre their attention on their own experiential learning... to direct their attention to processes which are taking place within them. Thus you can induce a trance by directing patients' attention to experiences, to memories, to ideas, to concepts that belong to them. All you do is direct the patients' attention to those processes within themselves."[4]

A focused state of attention can come about in a number of ways, each of which has a direct bearing on the type and/or quality of trance state.

The most basic trance state (which we share with animals[5]) occurs when we get highly emotional and, as a consequence, see reality from only one particular perspective. The emotional brain takes over and we focus on what has aroused us, to the increasing exclusion of other inputs. In this type of trance state the higher cortex is less engaged in reality checking.[6] You can clearly see this when, for example, someone gets angry and you cannot reason with them. In anger a person is totally focused and incapable of seeing other points of view, and will appear stupid. We see this narrowed down, focused state happening in all instinct driven emotional states, including anxiety, fear, greed, aggression, lust and elation.

Another way we enter trance is when we *voluntarily* choose to focus our attention on something that interests us. If we are intensely interested in football, for example, and choose to watch a game, we get absorbed. Again, although voluntarily entered into, this state involves emotional arousal as the fortunes of the teams fluctuate. So this could also be described as an emotionally induced trance state – but deliberately engendered by oneself. Indeed, any good observer of their own and other people's behaviour will recognise that *any* form of absorbing activity entered into voluntarily is trance inducing: reading, music, athletic activity, sexual behaviour, dancing, concentration on ideas, watching something closely and so on.

But there is yet another trance state that is fundamentally entwined in our lives and behaviour – the one produced when somebody *else* focuses our attention. This, too, is one of nature's amazing solutions to a primary survival need we all share. Without it we could not absorb family and cultural norms, relate to other people or live in inter-connected groups. Why this is so will become clear later.

Mothers are instinctively expert at focusing young children's attention. Good teachers focus the attention of children, the friend or raconteur in the pub focuses our attention, as does a good salesman and the leaders who arise in society. When this is done to us we can be deemed to be in a trance state. This is because, when our attention is guided, certain aspects of reality are left out and certain courses of action are made more compelling to us by the person organising the presentation of the evidence, or story, that we are hearing. To the extent that they succeed in focusing our attention in a way that we accept, we are suggestible. So trance states can be created between people simply by another person focusing our attention.

Then there is the type of trance state that is the subject matter of the article in the *New Scientist* – the one that the hypnotist or hypnotherapist supposedly creates. On one side of the debate people want to say that there *is* something unusual about this trance state and, on the other, people are saying that this is no different from the suggestibility that occurs in everyday life, such as we have described above.

To some extent both parties are right. Whilst dreaming at night, for example, we might vividly experience ourselves in a field of snow, even though we are actually tucked up in our warm beds. When we dream, we are creating an alternative reality *in our imagination*. This can be thought of as being done by the brain's own 'reality simulator'.[7] Even when not in a dream state some people are quite good at visualising what it would be like to be in a field of snow – the whiteness, intense cold and so on. So we are not, in that sense, doing something extraordinary when we go into an hypnotic trance because every night, in our dream state, we totally believe in the alternative reality our brain presents to us – we can actually *feel* we are in a field of snow. We limit our normal waking reality testing processes to such an extent that we totally accept the dream vision of reality.

The trance state of dreaming and the role of metaphor

In dreaming we have an example of the trance state par excellence. It is the deepest trance state we know of. When we dream, not only is our attention being directed in a non-voluntary fashion, but an alternative visionary reality is created that, ninety-nine percent of the time, we totally accept whilst in the dream. This is so every night for all of us. (It can occasionally happen, of course, that a person becomes aware that they are dreaming – lucid dreaming).

Most of the people who say that trance states don't exist will nevertheless agree that we dream and that dreaming is a separate state from waking consciousness. They will also acknowledge (because there is so much evidence for it) that, in the dream state, the emotional brain is firing off on all cylinders and generating the dreams. This has repeatedly been demonstrated in sleep laboratories.[8] In dreaming the emotional brain is very much in control, and that gives us a strong clue as to how and why trance states evolved in the first place. They are connected to emotions.

It can also be shown from other research that the Rapid Eye Movement (REM) state during which dreaming takes place is involved with programming instinctive frames of references into our brain.[9] That's another vital clue.

Instinctive behaviours are inherited patterns which allow a prepared response to anticipated stimuli which an animal can expect to encounter in its future environment.[10] The important point to note is that the anticipated stimuli *can have their parameters only partially specified* in order to allow for the range of variation which individual members of a species may expect to encounter within their habitat. This is because the genetic description of specifically anticipated stimuli has to allow for the range of variation that will be encountered within specific stimuli. The more unspecified the parameters of genetically anticipated stimuli (and responses as well), the greater will be the flexibility in the animal's behaviour, and the greater can be the environmental learning component of the instinctive behaviour. In other words, the more metaphorical ability is built into a creature, the more flexibly it can operate and evolve.

Metaphorical communication is an intrinsic part of the way human beings understand and communicate experience. Metaphorical expression always occurs in dreams and is far more widespread in our waking lives than most of us realise. This is particularly important for therapists to understand because, just as we have the potential to identify appropriate metaphors, we may also make inappropriate metaphorical matches between two patterns. In fact error is inevitable on some occasions because the capacity for analogy or metaphor *derives biologically from the programming of instinctive behaviour.* Instinctive templates for behaviour can only specify patterns to be identified in an approximate way. Consider how many mammals use their unique vocal patterns for the mutual recognition of parent and young. The genetic schema cannot include the specific voice pattern that a particular parent or baby will have, only the likely range. This has to be so in order to allow animals the flexibility of response they need to survive. That's how metaphorical processes came into being.

Many people have seen film of the ethologist Konrad Lorenz being followed around everywhere by a family of young goslings. Goslings are preprogrammed to attach themselves to the first large moving object they encounter after hatching because, normally, this would be their mother. Now, if that large moving object is Konrad Lorenz and they attach to him and not the mother goose, clearly the wrong metaphorical patterns have been identified. The birds bonded with Lorenz, they followed him persistently, they became distressed when he left them and ran to him for support when they felt frightened.[11] Clearly this is a situation where the matching of an instinctive template to its environmental counterpart has gone awry.

Human beings have a far more sophisticated, creative capacity for identifying metaphor than do animals, but it stems directly from the metaphorical processes found throughout the animal kingdom. We have the ability to think *analogically*, that is, to think holistically, and to recognise how a pattern metaphorically matches another pattern. But we also have the ability to think *logically*, to break problems down and analyse them. Our conscious mind's preferred mode of operation is logical thought while that of our unconscious mind is analogical or 'association of ideas', as it is sometimes called.

A great many mental problems are caused by these thinking processes going awry. When someone who has been sexually abused in a past relationship, for example, finds that they cannot bring themselves to have sex with their present partner, whom they love, they are making a false analogical connection between the old abusive relationship and the new healthy one. It is a form of learned helplessness that the logical conscious mind seems powerless to overcome but that hypnotherapists have great success with. Another example of false analogy matching is when a person is highly aroused early in their sexual life and makes associations between that arousal and particular objects, activities or situations. They then continue to be sexually 'turned on' by such connections (fetishism) which can seem inexplicably perverse to others. From this perspective the goslings following Lorenz's wellington boots are perverts.

When people are suffering from inappropriate patterns established in the past they may need help to unhook themselves from the past patterns so they can be fully in the present. By using hypnosis this is not difficult to do in therapy. But therapy that just encourages an emotional re-experiencing of the past problem has the undesired effect of enhancing the mismatch – engraining the inappropriate pattern deeper and harming the patient.

Evolutionary pressures leading to REM sleep

It was professor Michel Jouvet who first suggested that REM sleep, which is so closely linked to dreaming and trance states, may have evolved to permit more freedom in the expression of instinctive behaviour.[12] To understand how central this is to our understanding of the complexity of human psychology and the link between dreaming and hypnosis we need to take a brief look at the evolutionary pressures that led to the emergence of REM sleep.

The ability of mammals and birds to keep a constant internal temperature conferred great advantages on them in terms of mobility. But there was a great price to pay – more than a fivefold increase in basic energy expenditure over cold-blooded creatures.[13] Such a massive increase in metabolism was compensated for by a corresponding increase in the requirement for energy. It made no sense to meet this requirement by simply extending the time spent looking for food. What was needed was a matching increase in productivity, a more productive return between the energy expended in seeking food and the energy gained by acquiring it. One part of this came from cutting down on wasteful time, for example, sleeping when prey or other sources of food were not available. This can be seen as one of the functions of 'slow wave' sleep. But, if one reduces energy expenditure by cutting out nonproductive time, although this does conserve energy, it doesn't actually provide any.

Since a massive increase in energy gain is required to compensate for the demands of being warm blooded there was clearly a need to develop the ability to employ this new, high-powered energy system in more productive ways. Essentially the animal needed to become more intelligent, hence the expansion of the neocortex in mammals. This enables the animal to inhibit certain drives if their attempted expression is deemed unlikely to be successful, and thus avoids wasting precious energy. Equally, if the neocortex's analysis shows that a certain course of action is likely to bring results, it can promote such action by stimulating expectation. This, of course, is the function ascribed to the greatly expanded neocortex in mammals. MacLean summed this up well when he wrote: "A remarkable feature of the neocortex is that it evolved primarily in relation to systems receiving and processing information from the external world, namely the exteroceptive, visual, auditory and somatic systems. It was as though the neocortex was designed to serve as a more objective intelligence in coping with the external environment."[14]

For this objective intelligence to operate, it must have a detailed knowledge of, or access to, information about the instinctive programmes. If these instinctive programmes are to allow for individual and environmental variation, then this involves incompletely specified models for which sensory analogues have to be environmentally identified. It seems that the function of REM sleep in the foetus and neonate is the programming of these genetically anticipated patterns of stimulation. And, because they are necessarily incomplete, they can only be expressed metaphorically. The programming must carry the instruction to find the matching environmental stimuli to complete the template – be it language, sexual stimuli or prey for food etc.[15]

Why we evolved to dream

Nature still had one more problem to solve. This is that, once an instinct driven pattern is activated, it can normally only be deactivated by the actual carrying out of the programmed behaviour by the central nervous system and this clearly does not give animals the flexibility they need to survive. We can see this easily in our own lives. When you get annoyed with your children, for example, and tell them off or smack them this usually dissipates your anger. But, if you bottle it up the anger is still retained in the nervous system. If every time we were emotionally aroused we were to act out those emotions it would be disastrous. There would be continuous violent and sexual mayhem for a start. Furthermore, if we could only inhibit arousals without dealing with them in some way, we would require an enormously larger brain than would be feasible. So animals needed to evolve the ability to inhibit the arousals when necessary and deactivate them later when they could do no harm. That's why we evolved to dream.[16] During REM sleep activated instinct drive patterns 'left over' from waking are vicariously run out, thus deactivating them and releasing the data processing potential of the neocortex to deal with the emotionally arousing contingencies of the next period of being awake.

Thus we can see the beautiful economy of nature. The same process that programmes instinctive behaviour – the genetically anticipated patterns of stimulation – are also used to deactivate 'left over' anticipated patterns of stimulation from waking – the activated instinctive drive patterns. The instinctive frames of reference programmed in REM sleep don't have sensory content until they are matched up with their environmental counterparts. The anticipated or introspected stimulation which gives rise to dreaming on the other hand, does contain a sensory description and thus its analogical processing in REM sleep – dreaming. Thus nature accomplishes two essential functions with the same process.

A puzzle solved

The two major types of trance states are:
- post hypnotic trance states
- programming trance states.

We see both of them within the REM state in animals and humans. During early life in the womb, the foetus is preprogrammed in the REM state as to how to interpret reality in different circumstances and stages of life.[17] Then, whenever that programming is activated, our genes stimulate us to become emotional.[18] And, when the instinctive basis of behaviour is activated, our attention is focused again and we are in the equivalent of a post hypnotic trance state. Suppose you tell a good hypnotic subject that later (after they come out of hypnosis), when they hear the clock strike three, they are going to feel an itch on their forehead and scratch it. When the clock strikes three, it activates that programming and they scratch themselves. They are not aware of it when they are doing it but, nonetheless, their behaviour is controlled by a post hypnotic programme.

Similarly when you get angry and feel that somebody is trespassing on your rights, you may suddenly strike out or hit somebody, or say something in an involuntary way. When you calm down, you will say, "Why the hell did I do that...? What came over me...?" But, nonetheless, at the time you felt compelled to act as you did, just as a person is compelled to act from a post hypnotic suggestion. This is an important similarity.

What needs to be understood by the scientific community, before it can make further progress in studying hypnosis, is this: whilst trance *is* tapping in to the same mechanism that the salesman and everybody else uses, if we *deliberately* put a person who is a good hypnotic subject into an hypnotic state, we are activating the same processes that the brain itself activates during dream sleep, including the brain's astonishing and powerful reality simulator. It is often observed that a deeply hypnotised person can hallucinate all kinds of realities, depending on their hypnotic ability and the skill of the hypnotist.[19] They will hallucinate to the same degree of intensity that would occur in a dream state and, whilst in the trance, have the same degree of belief in its being real. It is only with the breakthrough in our understanding of the origin of dreams that this insight has become possible.[20] We now know that the dream is like a script that is processed in metaphorical imagery by the reality simulator that is the REM state. In hypnosis we are directly accessing this reality simulator and the hypnotist is providing the script.

But there is more to it than that. When the dream state naturally occurs, the person's body is normally paralysed, all muscle tone disappearing as the dreamer switches off outside perceptions of reality in order to focus on the inward reality. So there are physiological similarities between the dream state and what can be activated in the hypnotic state – and that *is* different from being absorbed by the salesman's hypnotic patter. Trance is clearly a matter of degree. Its characteristics change, just as water can change – it can solidify into ice or evaporate. What you can do with ice is quite different from what you can do with steam, but it is water all the same and retains its fundamental quality.

So, when we've got the person into an hypnotic state and they are imagining fields of snow or whatever, the skilled hypnotist can, in a good subject, evoke other physiological similarities with the REM state, such as paralysis of the body. These may even occur in some people spontaneously. And because the body in the REM state naturally shuts out sensory information it is easy, for example, to block out pain, alter sensory perceptions or, as some stage hypnotists do, convince people that intimate parts of their body are missing. All this leads to confusion about what a trance state is.

The trance state that the good salesman creates is hypnotic; the trance state of getting somebody to imagine something, an alternative reality, is also hypnotic. But, with a good trance subject, you can alter their perceptions through changing their physiological state. In all these cases what you are doing is evoking the latent abilities that are naturally present in the REM state, namely, shutting out certain physiological sensations and changing a person's perception so that one part of the brain takes in information while another part of the brain blocks it. This also occurs spontaneously during the dream state because a person can call or shout to you when you're dreaming, yet your brain may ignore it; though sometimes certain information does filter through and can affect the content of dreams. So there is a blockage, or partial blockage, on outside information getting into the dream state just as there is in hypnosis.

In hypnosis subjects can be made to alter their blood pressure, stimulate their immune system and other remarkable and well-documented things.[21] But even this has parallels with dreaming in the REM state. Who has not woken up, heart pounding, sweating and flushed from an arousing dream or a nightmare that has had strong physiological effects? And the immune system's healing response is known to be more highly active during periods of right hemispherical dominance during the day and night[22] and it is the right hemisphere that is dominant in dreaming and trance.[23]

So now we can see that many of the strange and seemingly bizarre phenomena evoked during hypnosis are quite normal when you consider them as REM state activity. Once it's understood that all we are doing in hypnosis is evoking the latent capacities of the REM state, the strange mystery of hypnosis – pain control, dissociation, hallucination, alterations of perception, paralysis etc – no longer baffles ... it's a puzzle solved.

Even the fact that we mostly forget our dreams, unless we make a conscious effort to fix them in our consciousness by telling them back to ourselves immediately on waking, is paralleled with the common experience of amnesia for hypnotic experiences.

Posthypnotic suggestions and the REM state

It's curious that we forget our dreams so easily when we wake up but, later in the day, something can trigger a memory of a dream. The dream template only comes back when it recognises a pattern in the environment that relates closely to it. This

---

*When we access the REM state in ways other than during dreaming we don't see the usual brain pattern associated with the REM state because the state is now being induced, not *internally* by the lower brain stem and through the PGO orientation response, but through the *external* focusing of attention. The orientation response prepares the organism to respond to what may be significant new stimuli. Perception is a constructive process and hence we sometimes misperceive people and things – mistakenly thinking we recognise someone, or see objects and shapes that turn out to be different from what we first thought they were. A figure lying in the road on closer inspection can turn out to be a bag of rubbish. In other words, perception is our best informed guess at what we think we are seeing or hearing in a given situation. During sleep, the PGO spikes, as part of an endogenously produced orientation response pattern (see next page), alert the organism to process information regarding significant new stimuli. In fact, of course, sensory information from outside is actively inhibited when we sleep. In the absence of outside information, the brain can only base its 'best guess' on significant information that it is actively anticipating – the activated pattern of emotional arousal – and hence these are released during REM sleep and analogically processed as real perceptions. These are our dreams.

may be connected to post hypnotic functions because it is a misconception that sleep is the exclusive medium for the REM state. The REM state can be accessed in other ways*, such as during the directing of attention in an hypnotic induction. As we have seen, in dreaming the REM state is activated spontaneously to deal with unresolved emotional arousals from the previous waking period. When these arousals are released they spontaneously trigger off the REM state.

Research by Milton Erickson[24], for example, showed that, when a person who has been given a post hypnotic suggestion is carrying it out, if you interrupt them and give them another suggestion, they respond to the new suggestion too. In other words, they are actually in a trance whilst carrying out the suggestions and are not aware that they are.

So any time we become emotional or are acting through instinct, we are in a trance state where we are more easily programmed. At such times our attention can be diverted and

---

PGO spikes

The visual brain stimulates itself in REM sleep through a mechanism reflected in EEG recordings as PGO waves. These electrical signals originate in the pons (P) from the neurones that move the eyes and are then conducted to both the lateral geniculate (G) body in the thalamus and to the occipital cortex (O) - hence PGO spikes.

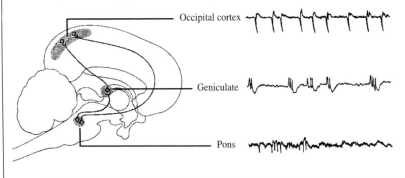

Occipital cortex

Geniculate

Pons

---

somebody can take control over aspects of our behaviour. That's what all dictators, evangelists and salesmen do; they have learned how to raise people's emotional pitch so as to focus their listeners in a particular direction, influencing them to their own ends.

In charismatic 'religious' healing services, for example, the emotional temperature is first raised, automatically putting people into trance states. They are then more suggestible and it is quite an easy matter to invoke, for example, the blocking of pain through dissociation. Members of the congregation can feel their pain diminish and believe that cures are effected, (as they *can* be with psychosomatic problems) and, if the leaders are unscrupulous, experience a compelling urge to part with lots of money.

It is because of this confusion between the idea of trance states, which are essentially post hypnotic – emotional states in which we act from frames of reference in the emotional brain – and the physiological correlates of the trance state which can be activated in hypnosis, namely dissociation, amnesia, anaesthesia etc., that some people have the impression that hypnosis is an unusual altered state of consciousness. It is not. It is an essential, everyday part of being human, one of what some psychologists now call the 'human givens'[25], our natural inheritance of behaviour and mind/body functioning.

An interesting aspect of all this is that, whilst carrying out a post hypnotic suggestion, we look absolutely normal, even though we are, effectively, in the dream state. Scientific observers are not easily going to admit that people are in some altered state of consciousness. Yet when *you* have been inside the dream state and recall it, you *know* that you were in an altered state of consciousness because *you did* experience an alternate reality.

Suppose very few people actually remembered their dreams. It would be difficult to prove that the dream state existed. But we know that dreaming *is* a separate state of consciousness, even though the brainwave pattern whilst dreaming is almost identical to when we are wide awake.

So it is impossible to satisfy the requirement of people who want to show that hypnotic states are an altered state of consciousness unique to hypnosis sessions. They have set themselves up for failure because trance states occur in all kinds of situations, including, and especially, while we sleep.

Hypnotherapy and expectation

It is, of course, important for people to know that trances are states of focused attention that we are all going in and out of all of the time. But people who use hypnosis deliberately are often going for something extra – therapy. In good subjects we can trigger the physiological equivalent of the REM state, namely shutting out pain, shutting out physiological perceptions and causing disassociations. That is one of the most powerful and useful things that the deliberate use of hypnosis can do. People still doubt it happens but, once experienced, perhaps by having a pain free operation under hypnosis, it is impossible to deny.

To the degree we have expectations about anything, our consciousness is being shaped by those expectations. This means that in everyday life we are continuously in trance but to varying depths because our expectation is selectively focusing our attention, thus always preventing us from seeing the bigger picture – what's really there. And, to the degree that we are even more involved in our expectations, we are more emotionally aroused. This is easy to observe when someone is about to meet a famous person – the Queen, a pop star or politician – they are in a trance, their attention is completely focused. This is why bizarre behaviour such as sycophancy so often occurs around such meetings.

It has long been observed that expectation can play an important role in hypnotic induction (although it is not an essential element since people can unwittingly be hypnotised). When we observe the effect of expectation about what trance is, we can see highlighted the nature of the trance state itself. This is because the REM state is a reality simulator and will tend to fulfil the expectations that a person has about trance. If the person associates trance with relaxation, for example, then the REM state has the capacity to produce relaxation and so they will experience relaxation. In contrast, children, who tend not to have preconceptions about trance states, tend to be much more mobile during trance. They don't associate hypnosis with relaxation so they can be more active when in a trance.

Ernest Rossi, who has done much to familiarise the world with the work of Milton Erickson, once said at a seminar that one of the best ways to get people into a trance state is to have them observing someone else go into one first. By the process of observation their expectations about going into trance are heightened and it is then much easier to work with them. This is as one would expect because, when attention is being focused and emotion aroused, people are already highly suggestible. By the time they sit in the hypnotherapist's chair to be hypnotised they are already in a trance.

There is an interesting phrase used in Ireland to describe people who have had a lot to drink. They say, "he was really 'locked' last night!" What it means is that the drinker's consciousness was locked into a certain perspective. He was in the trance state of wanting to drink and that was the only reality that existed for him for a while. The outside world and outside responsibility did not exist at all and all he wanted to do was keep that state going until he fell over.

The phrase 'your conscious mind is locked' is descriptive of what a trance state is. In trance consciousness *is* locked because it is focused. Now this happens every day to all of us in different ways and to different degrees. To say that this is something extraordinary and unique to hypnosis is quite false because it is not. Just as we can recognise the dream reality from within, we can recognise the state of consciousness of being 'locked'. Hypnotherapists are aware that the hypnotic subject's attention *is* locked since an unexpected sudden bang or noise that makes the hypnotist jump has no effect on the subject in trance.

We have no doubt though that, as our physiological monitoring instruments become more subtle, there will be even more physiological indices of the trance state of hypnosis existing. As we mentioned at the start, with people who are hypnotised to feel no pain, for example, we can see on PET scans that they are activating the parts of the brain that block out perceptions of pain (something people trying to fake being hypnosised cannot do[26]).

Scientific study of hypnosis

It is clear that an understanding of how emotions work, how genetic programming takes place and how the imaginative mind can be focused by other people, is a prerequisite for understanding hypnosis. We hope that we have made it clear that hypnosis is not something separate from ordinary daily life. It is an intrinsic part of it: a reality that can quite easily be understood with the right organising idea.

Of course many scientists researching hypnosis naturally want to follow the traditional, ritualistic protocol that scientists working in other areas usually use. But these fixed and mechanistic tools of investigation are not always suitable for studying human consciousness and attention – as shown by what happened in the early days of clinical research into the subject. Absurd conclusions were reached about hypnosis because experimenters were using scripts to hypnotise people. Those who did not respond were described as unhypnotisable or bad hypnotic subjects.

Good hypnotists flexibly use their subjects' own interests, creative imagination and behavioural traits to induce trance. Hypnotic ability varies enormously from individual to individual but, sooner or later, with enough time, *anyone* with normal brain functioning can be induced into a trance. Some people can be hypnotised by a mechanically read hypnotic script but more subtlety is required with the majority, as Erickson and others have shown.

The crude nature of scientific research procedures in this area stops many scientists from thinking clearly. One of the mistakes that many of those who deny the reality of hypnosis make is that they define hypnosis as the state which is induced by a specific type of induction process that they put people through. Then they find that other people who are good hypnotic subjects can be put into a similar state of consciousness without that induction and conclude therefore that induction is not necessary, so therefore hypnosis doesn't exist. They then go on to say the terms hypnosis and trance are redundant.[27] We believe, however, that the words 'hypnosis' and 'trance' are useful and should not be abandoned because scientists disagree as to how and when they should be used. Lay people can accurately identify trance states in themselves and other people, and we know that hypnotic inductions and trance phenomena have been the subject of serious experiment for thousands of years in various cultures, resulting in highly sophisticated therapeutic effects.[28]

Moreover we have a need for trance, as can be seen by the way we seek out experiences that put us into it. Golfers, for example, will say, "I just find it so relaxing, that's why I play. I come out here and I can switch off everything else. Nothing exists for me then but the game."

It is as if, for all of us, our consciousness – the constant switching of attention that enables us to see reality in multi dimensions as much as possible – is a real burden we carry around. Every time we switch attention we arouse, to some degree, the fight or flight response and activate a corresponding amount of stress hormones.[29] That creates tremendous wear and tear.[30] But, when we can go into a relaxed, absorbing trance state and our attention is kept focused, the fight or flight response is subdued.[31] Perhaps, without realising it, we are all looking for experiences where we can put the burden down and thereby avoid using energy to make the necessary effort of emotional arousal needed for constantly switching attention.

It's impossible to be anxious and relaxed at the same time. Relaxation is a lovely state to be in. It's entrancing! It's what a lot of people get out of drinking alcohol – their attention and consciousness gets 'locked', so they don't need to make much effort. This temporarily filters out certain stress reactions which would otherwise affect their mind/body system. It's a phoney freedom of course. You cannot escape reality for long.

Playing squash or badminton will do the same thing. No matter what problems you have or what deadlines there are, once you start playing the game you are totally released, everything else just disappears for an hour. You almost become unconscious for while. The only thing that matters is the game, nothing else. The wider reality is temporarily forgotten and it's a refreshing release from day to day pressures. Whilst playing sport does involve physiological activation of the fight or flight response there is an instinctive follow-through, when one can play well, that switches off that arousal so we don't have the conscious decision-making associated with it. That's why it seems so effortless... going into a state of 'flow' involves very little conscious decision making.

Depressed people stop doing things they used to enjoy, so they no longer have that release. Once trapped in a negative (unhelpful) trance state they lose the energy required to focus themselves on a wider horizon, one that has meaning and purpose.

The trance of depression[32] is quite unlike the trance of playing badminton for example which, by contrast, is an exhilarating state. That's because, when playing, you are totally focused, but *outwards*, not *inwards*. And what you are not doing when in that outward focused trance is carrying the burden ... decisions to be made, deadlines to be met ... all the things which happen in life which require consciousness, choices and reality checking. We may try to escape the burden through negative trance states. We become lazy, dreamy, depressed, anxious or angry. We abuse substances or excitement or relationships – do anything, in fact, except take up the burden willingly. When we focus outwards, as in sport, music and other activities requiring concentration, we are relieved of the burden for a while in a much less destructive manner.

We may not like the burden. But equally, getting caught up in a negative trance state also becomes a burden because, after a certain length of time, we start to get bored with it. We start to realize that there are all kinds of pleasures we are no longer having and suddenly our life becomes meaningless. It's like becoming aware that you are dreaming the same dream over and over to a point where it becomes boring. If you stay in a trance state, a part of the mind eventually becomes aware of it and how repetitive it is. You begin to think, "I'm not doing anything interesting in my life, in fact my life is boring. I'm not enjoying my food as much as I used to, I have no energy ... this is going to go on forever." Then the trance state itself becomes a burden, and one sinks into depression.

In the depression trance, the patient is in a highly aroused emotional state, endlessly ruminating over their concerns. Emotional arousal, as we have seen, leads to locked-in, simplified, black and white thinking, which can make situations seem much more hopeless than they really are.

A further consequence of the excessive negative rumination that takes place in depression is that it leads to excessive REM sleep. Ordinarily the right amount of REM sleep brings our arousal levels back down to normal, but the pathological proportion of REM sleep seen in depressed people leaves them waking up exhausted each morning. (All therapies that successfully lift depression do so by reducing REM sleep. For a detailed description of this process see our monograph, *Breaking the cycle of depression.*[33])

It should be clear now that, once we understand what a trance state is and the various ways it can be induced, we have a useful way of observing and explaining much of our behaviour.

We love many types of positive trance experiences that externally focus our attention, for example, precisely because they take us away from the business of continuously maintaining multiple focuses of attention, with all the associated physiological arousal and effort that requires. It *is* lovely to switch off.

Uses and abuses of hypnosis

There is often confusion, in literature on the subject, about the apparently weird things (hallucination, loss of sensory feeling, paralysis, regression etc.) that happen in hypnotic states. These phenomena are easily understood, however, once it is realised that the hypnotist is actually activating the machinery of the dream state itself. Dreaming is concerned with our emotional and physical health, deactivating unresolved emotional arousals from the daytime and, whilst dreaming, we accept the often bizarre reality the brain presents us with in its endless flow of metaphorical activity. The metaphorical happenings in dreams, of course, are frequently bizarre but are accepted by us because we cannot reality-check them. We totally accept the reality of the dream while we are still dreaming, however odd it may be. And this is what can happen too in stage hypnosis.[34] The most outrageous suggestions can be played out when the dream mechanism is activated by the hypnotist and can be intensely meaningful for the subject – until he 'wakes up'.

Just as dream language is always metaphorical[35] so using metaphor is central to hypnotherapy.[36] The use of metaphor is at the heart of good therapeutic practice as repeatedly demonstrated by Milton H. Erickson and the many others who learnt from him.

But hypnosis does not only help us create alternate 'realities', as in dreams, it also makes it possible for us to bring about changes to our bodies. It can promote healing in skin and bones, reduce blood pressure, change the experience of pain, improve digestion and so on. There is nothing remarkable about all this when one sees the larger picture. In the dream state, for example, we switch off sensory perceptions, the body is paralysed. So, when a hypnotist tells you "you can't get out of your chair" and you say, "I'm stuck to the chair", it's not magic, because we are all stuck for about two hours every night – when we're paralysed during REM sleep.

But some people have a terrible fear that a hypnotist can take control from them with some magical power. It is not magical, but the hypnotist *does* have power. This is because he is providing a dream script for your brain to work on and this is a serious form of influence. Therefore great caution is needed – power can be corrupting. For many hundreds of years Eastern psychologists who have studied it have warned about the harm that can be done to human development by the ignorant or unscrupulous use of hypnosis. We have seen the truth of this in tragic cases involving the generation of illusory memories of sexual abuse and multiple personalities by therapists and the concern about the accidental triggering of schizophrenia in people by stage hypnotists.

We need to be clear about what is and what is not potentially harmful in the use of hypnosis. It is safe to evoke the natural anaesthesia that accompanies the REM state to carry out operations without chemical anaesthesia. It is safe to detraumatize a traumatic memory using hypnosis. It is safe to use guided imagery to suggest life enhancing alterations to a hypnotised subject. However, if we use hypnosis so that post hypnotically a person experiences the integration of normal reality and an imaginary reality, then we are manipulating the very frames of reference through which that person's reality is experienced. This is potentially very harmful. In a subject who has a predisposition to confuse 'normal' frames of reference and imagination such an experience could facilitate a psychotic breakdown. Since the precursor for such psychotic breakdown is often stress, if the recollection of the hypnotically induced 'psychotic' experience were also to prove stressful then this would further increase the likelihood of damage to the subject's ability to separate fantasy from reality. Such procedures are, of course, the very stuff of stage hypnosis which must, therefore, carry a risk of triggering psychotic states in vulnerable individuals. If hypnosis can be used to facilitate a more sane and orderly perception of reality, then its misuse also carries a negative potential to facilitate a disordered perception of reality.

There are also potential dangers attached to simply suggesting symptoms away, which is of course possible in a good hypnotic subject. This is because we may disturb the balance between various feedback loops within the psyche to the detriment of the overall functioning of the personality. Clearly we need to be more subtle. If, for example, we teach the client an alternative way to meet the need fulfilled by the symptom; or if we help the client to see that their perception was biased, this is a much more sophisticated approach that is likely to have beneficial results.

Some people might wonder why nature has made our brain and behaviour so open to influence? After all, we keep telling ourselves that the human brain is the most intelligent and complex organ that exists in the universe, but this is surely a major defect if other people can take it over and alter its functioning so easily? But, once you understand that hypnosis *is accessing that programme of the REM state which is absolutely vital for life itself* – for programming our instinctive knowledge and the acting out of it through post hypnotic suggestion – then you realise that hypnosis is tapping into the most basic programme of all. A programme without which we couldn't exist. So potent is this mechanism that our highest achievements, and civilization itself, grew out of it.

All of us have, and retain, a propensity to be programmed by other people and by the wider culture. All of us are, in fact, conditioned. We take on the values and belief systems of our culture.[37] Our politics, religion and moral values are an accident of birth. However, whilst programming/conditioning is a valuable mechanism enabling us to survive wherever in the world we are born, there are also great dangers associated with it. This is because it seems natural to us to act out that programming. It's the most natural thing in the world to believe in the value system, and religious or cultural ideals we are brought up with. But we may end up not standing back and realising that we are programmed, never questioning those values and therefore never seeing beyond the 'truth' of our own culture. All cultures are relative and see reality differently and are biased or prejudiced in favour of certain aspects of reality, while omitting others. The process conditions us, limiting our options, and, in addition, certain elements in society can take advantage of that mechanism – sales people, dictators, cult leaders, trivialisers – and actually preoccupy or even enslave us. We need, as a culture, to be more aware of this.[38]

The fact that we are so easily conditioned explains why so many people have a need for psychotherapy. They accept the models they have been conditioned into by their family and, where their family is dysfunctional, it's difficult for them to spot the maladaptive patterns that they are operating from without the help of a therapist.

Fortunately therapists have an ally in nature which has provided us with a mechanism for making it possible to step outside our conditioning. It is variously called 'the observing self', 'the transparent centre', and 'that which is aware'.[39]

The observing self

Our 'observing self' is the natural opposite of the trance state. When our 'observing self' is activated we have stepped back from our trance state and thus widened the focus of our attention so that reality can be observed from more than one viewpoint. Traditional Eastern psychology has long taught the art of flexible disengagement from emotional trance states so that the world can be seen more objectively. It is only when we are in our observing self that we can actually question our own conditioning. This is because the observing self is a more fundamental part of us than even our thinking and feeling selves. It is our awareness which everything else feeds into. A person could lose arms, legs, sight, hearing and yet still have that sense of 'I am', being a centre of experience of reality – 'I am aware'. The observing self supersedes thought, feeling and action *because it experiences these functions*. As Dr Arthur Deikman, who coined the term, says, "No matter what takes place, no matter what we experience, nothing is as central as the self that observes ... It is incapable of being objectified; whatever you can notice or conceptualise is already an object of awareness, not awareness itself. Unlike every other aspect of experience – thoughts, emotions, desires and functions – the observing self can be known but not located, known but not 'seen'."

As Deikman further points out, "The observing self is not part of the object world formed by our thoughts and sensory perceptions because, literally, it has no limits; everything else does. Thus, everyday consciousness contains a transcendent element that we seldom notice because that element is the very ground of our experience. The word *transcendent* is justified because, if subjective consciousness – the observing self – cannot itself be observed but remains forever apart from the contents of consciousness, it is likely to be of a different order from everything else. Its fundamentally different nature becomes evident when we realise that the observing self is featureless; it cannot be affected by the world any more than a mirror can be affected by the images it reflects."[40]

The evolution of the observing self in human beings is possibly the most important distinction between us and the rest of the animal kingdom. This was first recognised by Eastern psychology but only in the last two decades is it beginning to be incorporated into Western psychology. All good therapists have the skill to help a client step back into their observing self (even if they don't call it by that name) to identify the patterns of conditioning that need to change.

Hypnotic ability

Going in and out of trance stays with us as a need throughout our lives. When we give attention to people and receive attention we are going in and out of trance – internal focus, external focus, back and forth – and this serves a valuable need for us. It enables us to constantly stay in sync with the people around us, in our family, our society, our culture. If we didn't keep doing this, a process that paradoxically gives us flexibility, our own thought processes would get so bizarre that we would end up unable to operate within our culture. This is what happens to those people with various types of mental disorders. The thinking of lonely, isolated people becomes more unstable and bizarre. Normal people's thinking is stabilised and kept congruent with the models of our culture by going in and out of trance on a regular basis in the company of those around us. Whilst this is a great aid to keeping us sane, it is also our greatest weakness because the process limits our options.

This means that all the arguments about whether some

people are hypnotisable or not are irrelevant because *every* undamaged person has that process in them. We are all pre-programmed with instinctive templates and being activated by them – going in and out of trance all day long. We hypnotise each other to varying degrees many times on a daily basis. Such arguments are really only about how *some* hypnotists can't affect *some* people terribly well, for whatever reason. Erickson showed that you could eventually hypnotise everybody. Some-times he would take days over it but he did it. And somebody else, not Erickson, would have been able to put that "difficult" person in a trance straight away (perhaps his boss barking an order at him for example).

It is easy to hypnotise people when you understand the principle that it is simply a question of either mimicking the stages of relaxation before sleep, or any other part of the slide into the REM state programme. This can be done by forcing rapid eye movements by tracking a moving hand or pendulum, or by getting subjects to focus their attention in some way with all the creativity at your disposal. People can be hypnotised using their imagination, following a train of thought that you know they are intensively interested in, or by physical stimulus, sudden sound or shock. All have the common denominator of focusing attention. You just have to be flexible enough to find out what works with each individual.

Following is an example from one of us, Joe Griffin, who recently had a stressed man come to see him for hypnosis. "He was clearly embarrassed by the thought of hypnosis and when I started talking about relaxing, as soon as he felt himself relaxing, he started to giggle. Of course, as Erickson would have done, I said immediately that, 'one of the best ways to relax is to giggle. In fact, the more you giggle the more deeply relaxed you go, and if you try to stop it now you will find yourself compelled to giggle even more ...' and he started shaking with mirth! And I said 'I wouldn't be at all surprised now if you find that the shaking and giggling gets so intense that the shaking and giggling goes right down to your toes.' And it did! It was wonderful. Nevertheless I was holding his attention. The more he laughed the more he was allowing me to hold his attention. And that's all you need to do. If you can hold that attention mechanism for a minute or two minutes, the brain just assumes it is in some kind of a dream state and the neocortex surrenders power over to you, just as it surrenders two hours every night to allow itself to be directed by unresolved emotional arousals and dream them away.

"In the case of the giggling man I went from there into talking about his business and what he was doing in his business because that was also something that was intensely interesting to him. As I talked about that, I was keeping his attention even more focused. Once I had his attention focused for several minutes, he was in quite a profound, deep hypnotic state. In other words, his brain had actually allowed me to take over its attention directing mechanism and I could evoke all kinds of phenomena in him. After about half an hour, when he came out of trance, he had amnesia about everything that happened after the giggling. It was as remote to him as most dreams are and dreams are notoriously difficult to remember.

"I am quite certain that if he was being worked with in an experimental laboratory situation many scientists would have concluded that he was unhypnotisable because he couldn't stop giggling and the approach I used didn't conform to a 'standard procedure'. If I were following a script, it wouldn't have worked. You have to work with what is there."

It needs to be understood that there are people who surrender their ability to focus their attention more easily than others.

This is due partly to biological and partly to environmental factors. People who allow their attention to be focused easily *don't even need a trance induction.* You can say to them, "I want you to close your hand and when you try to open your hand you won't be able to open it", and they will respond to the suggestion. That's how some stage hypnotists select the people they are going to work with. Commonly they might say, "I want you all to put your hands tightly together and when I count to three your hands will be stuck together." They then pick out those in the audience who immediately responded to the suggestion. And these people have not had any form of induction.

So, if someone wants to prove that hypnosis doesn't exist, they will always be able to find people who will respond to a suggestion easily, enabling them to say that hypnosis is only suggestion. Conversely there are people who are so psychically defensive or left brain dominant, that reassurance, flexibility and creativity are required on the part of the hypnotist in order to get them to go into a trance.

A core study

The new knowledge about what hypnosis is and the role it plays in our lives, should enable hypnosis studies to move from being a peripheral esoteric mystery to being a core study with the potential to improve both our psychological understanding and our therapeutic practice. It is now time to put hypnosis and hypnotic phenomena where they belong, right at the centre of human psychology and our understanding of what it means to be human.

* * *

The authors of this paper would welcome views and
comment on it. Please write to:

Organising Ideas,
European Therapy Studies Institute (ETSI),
The Barn,
Church Farm,
Chalvington,
East Sussex
BN27 3TD

References

1. During a battle between the Imam Ali, cousin of Mohamed, and Amr Bin Wid, champion of the enemy host, Amr Bin Wid threw his amputated leg at Imam Ali before being killed.

2. *New Scientist* (4th, July 1998), No.2141.

3. *Science,* (1997), 277, p968.

4. Erickson, M.H. & Rossi, E.L. (1976) *Hypnotic Realities,* Irvington Publishers, New York.

5. We are not referring here to animal hypnosis, which is well documented elsewhere, but to experiments that show that, when animals get over-excited and are in a life threatening situation, they cannot see the obvious way out of their predicament in the same way that they can when they are not emotionally aroused. Spitz, R. (1965) *The First Year of Life,* International Universities Press, New York.

6. Golman, D. (1996). *Emotional Intelligence,* Bloomsbury Publishing.

7. Griffin, J. (1997). *The Origin of Dreams,* The Therapist Ltd.

8. Hobson, J.A. (1989) *Sleep,* Scientific American Library, a division of HPHLP, New York.

9. Jouvet, M. (1978) 'Does a genetic programming of the brain occur during paradoxical sleep?' P.A. Buser & A. Rougel-Buser (Eds.) *Cerebral Correlates of Conscious Experience,* Elsevier.

10. Piaget, J. (1971) *Biology and Knowledge,* Edinburgh University Press.

11. Lorenz, K.L. (1966) *On Aggression,* Methuen, London.

12. Jouvet, M. op. cit.

13. Karasov, W.H. & Diamond, J. (1985) *Digestive adaptations for fuelling the cost of endothermy.* Science, 228, 202-204.

14. Maclean, P.D. (1982) *Primate Brain Evolution: Methods and Concepts.* (Eds.) E. Armstrong & D. Folk, Plenum Publishing Corporation, 309.

15. Griffin, J. op. cit.

16. ibid.

17. ibid.

18. Joseph, R. (1993). *The limbic system and emotions "The Naked Neuron: Evolution and the Language of the Brain and Body",* Plenum Publishing

19. Yapko, M. (1990). *Trancework; An Introduction to the Practice of Clinical Hypnosis,* Brunner Mazel.

20. Griffin, J. op. cit.

21. Rossi, E.L. (1993) *The Psychobiology of Mind-Body Healing.* W.W. Norton.

22. Rossi, E.L. & Nimmons, D. (1991) *The 20 Minute Break,* Tarcher, Los Angeles.

23. ibid.

24. Rossi, E. L. (ed) (1989). *Collected papers of Milton H Erickson* (Vols. I, II, III & IV). Irvington Publishers, New York.

25. Griffin, J. & Tyrrell, I. (1998) *The Human Givens,* The Therapist, Vol. 5, No 1.

26. *Science,* (1997), 277, p968.

27. *Hypnosis in Europe,* (1998) Eds. Peter Hawkins, P. & Heap, M. Whurr.

28. Chester, R.J. *Hypnotism in the East and West,* Octagon, London

29. Morrison, A.R. (1983) *A Window on the Sleeping Brain.* Scientific American, *248, 86-94.*

30. Hobson, J.A. (1994) *The Chemistry of Conscious States,* Little Brown & Co, Canada.

31. ibid.

32. Yapko, M. (1992). *Hypnosis and the Treatment of Depressions.* Brunner Mazel, New York.

33. Griffin, J. and Tyrrell, I. (2000). *Breaking the Cycle of Depression,* ETSI Organising Ideas Monograph No. 3, HG Publishing.

34. McGill, O. (1996). *The New Encyclopedia of Stage Hypnotism,* Anglo American Book Company.

35. Griffin, J. op. cit.

36. Griffin, J. & Tyrrell, I. *The Metaphorical Mind: The Human Givens and the Evolution of Consciousness.* (In preparation.)

37. Shah, I (1994). *The Commanding Self,* Octagon Press.

38. Shah, I, (1998). *Knowing How to Know,* Octagon Press.

39. Deikman, A. J. (1982). *The Observing Self.* Beacon Press.

40. ibid. p. 95.

About the authors

JOE GRIFFIN is a psychologist with a thriving psychotherapy practice. Over the last decade thousands of health professionals have enjoyed his practical workshops and seminars on effective psychotherapy and counselling. He is widely recognised as one of the most informed and entertaining speakers on the subject having studied with many of the leading figures of the psychotherapy world. His other area of work is as a scientist and he spent 12 years researching why animals and humans evolved to dream. The resulting book which describes the breakthrough he made in this field, *The Origin of Dreams,* offered the first holistic synthesis – a recognition of the interdependence of the biological and the psychological – to explain the origin, function and meaning of dreams. His findings about mental processes have been described by scientific reviewers as, "the key to all psychic states ... an important milestone ... moves our understanding on significantly ... a watershed in our exploration of the evolution of mental processes." He is currently working on a new way of understanding evolutionary processes.

IVAN TYRRELL is a psychotherapist (specialising in brief therapy for depression and anxiety disorders) and a writer with a particular interest in the psychology of perception. He is a founder member of the European Therapy Studies Institute (ETSI) which, in 1992, launched *The Therapist* – the popular multi-disciplinary magazine for all caring professionals (now renamed *Human Givens: Radical Psychology Today*). His work for the *Human Givens* journal involves him in a continuing programme of writing, interviewing and invest-igating the latest developments in psychology, psychotherapy and the study of human behaviour. The *British Medical Journal* said of his book, *The Survival Option,* published by Jonathan Cape, "his practical information is reliable", and *The Times* wrote that it contained, "facts, not emotion... should be in every home in the country." Both he and Joe Griffin are members of the group involved with developing the human givens approach to applying knowledge of human psychology and behaviour to psychotherapy, counselling and education.